TABLE OF CONTENTS

INTRODUCTION

There are many definitions and ideas of what a homestead is. In a historical context, a "homestead" was defined as a parcel of land (typically 160 acres) that was granted to any US citizen willing to move West to settle on and farm the land for at least five years, as part of the Homestead Act of 1862.

In more modern terms, the act of homesteading is used to describe an agrarian and largely self-sufficient lifestyle. Homesteading activities typically include growing and preserving food crops, cooking meals from scratch, raising animals, making homemade medicines, personal care products, perhaps even clothing, and an overall goal to "live off the land". Homesteaders may also barter and trade for the things they cannot produce themselves.

Homesteaders come in many forms and styles these days. Some homesteaders have acres of land to play with (and maintain), while urban homesteaders are challenged and creative in smaller spaces. There are some hard-core, very traditional homesteaders that attempt to live a fully self-sufficient, zero-waste, off-grid, or near "prepper" status life. Then there are your hobby homesteaders, who are simply drawn to this lifestyle and enjoy it as a light-hearted escape from their usual 9-5 "real life". All versions of homesteading are awesome and acceptable! I'd say we are somewhere in between.

Keeping that in mind, let's see if we can help you better wrap your head around how to get started on your personal homesteading journey.

The Great Benefits of Homesteading (that we have found)

Note: This list is infinite and inexhaustible. But it'll at least give a taste of what we've experienced

Homesteading is a spectrum. Ultimately, the broadest definition is that it is a lifestyle with a commitment to self-sufficiency. This can encompass growing and preserving food; providing your own electricity with solar, wind or water; and even making your own fabric and clothing. Some homesteaders aspire never to use money; they want to make or barter for everything they need. Others may take a more measured approach, and although they aspire to provide as much as they can for themselves, they may be okay with using some money and working for pay—either as an end goal or during the transition to homesteading.

Urban and suburban homesteading is a subset of homesteading; people who live in the city or suburbs may still consider themselves homesteaders, and try to provide for their own needs within the confines of a small suburban house and yard or even a tiny city lot.

In the United Kingdom, "smallholding" is a similar term that means the same thing as homesteading—a goal of self-sufficiency, running a small, diversified farm that feeds the people who live on it.

WHY DO PEOPLE HOMESTEAD?

Homesteaders don't necessarily all share the same values and reasons for homesteading and can be a diverse bunch. Some may be retiring from a lucrative career that allows them to have the money to invest in the infrastructure needed to fully support themselves on the land. Others may be coming to homesteading with nothing, setting up a scrappy stronghold to provide for themselves in the face of economic hardship. These two situations could look very different, yet both people consider themselves homesteaders.

Homesteading is humbling:

As a homesteader, one quickly realizes just how small one is and how finite life is. For any homesteader, mistakes will be overwhelming. Animals will die. Crops will be ruined. Structures fall down. Plans fall through. It's humbling to attempt and tame a piece of this Earth, only to have it implode time after time. Which – hear me now – it will. The chickens may be eaten by an owl or the cow may stick her food in the milk bucket – but regardless of the failings that will inevitable come, homesteading continues. So while it may be an extremely humbling road to wander down, the perseverance bred through the humbling failures is not to be missed. It's character building, don't you think? To fail, recognize one's inability to control life, pray for grace, and then continue on.

Homesteading builds a strong work ethic:

Work ethic is something strongly missing in our culture, don't you think? I've recently been rereading Farmer Boy and am taken back by the amount of work that was expected of children. At the ripe 'ol age of six? seven? they're milking cows. Feeding animals. Training oxen. Cooking supper alongside their Mom. Kids are CAPABLE and thrive in such environments. While I'm thankful that our lifestyle no longer requires such labor from our children, it's important that the idea of building up ourselves (and our children) with strong work ethics isn't thrown out with the bathwater.

If anything will build up a solid work ethic, it's the responsibility that comes with growing food so that our family can EAT (ya. kinda important.) or raising animals that are reliant on us, day after day, for their survival.

The instant negativity associated with laziness in instantly felt on the homestead. The best way to breed it out is to slather it in work!

Homesteading tastes good!:

Many of y'all are chicken owners – you know the beautiful, orange, perky yolks that come from a well-loved and healthy hen. The taste is indistinguishable. I've ever surprised (why? I don't know) at the incredibly depth of difference of homegrown food to conventional food. Again, I think it's important to note: I'm very thankful that my survival is not dependent on my own ability to produce food. I think it's important and progressive that we have such food available to us year-round. But that being said, a lot of it just ain't good

Ever tasted an out-of-season-picked-green-raspberry? It's like a flavorless gob of nastiness.

Even my hard to convince husband was undoubtedly convinced at our last dinner date out – he ordered the roast chicken. "Well, it sure isn't like our Rainbow Rangers. It's sort of flat tasting and squishy." (You can read more about meat chickens here.) I felt the same about my steak, which was cooked and flavored beautifully, but still fell incredibly short of the grass-fed local meat we're used to. We spent the rest of the dinner planning how we could grow MORE of these things ourselves if for no other reason than the taste!

We're foodies. We like food that tastes the best.

And homegrown food tastes the best – fresh tomatoes from the summer garden, pastured eggs, homemade butter, fresh salsa, you name it. And I guarantee you it tastes better when you've grown it yourself.

I'd be hard pressed to find anyone who would disagree

Homesteading breeds appreciation:

Back to those fresh tomatoes. Remember the first one you ate out of your garden last year? I bet you do. Because before you could taste that first tomato, you had to put in months of work planting seeds, caring for tender seedlings, planning the proper time to plant them out, protecting them from harsh weather, nurturing them as they grew and blossomed, trellising them as they became heavy with fruit, and patiently waiting for them finally ripen. And when that first delicious orb is removed from the vine, it's hard to not be brought to tears. I guarantee you that after hand milking a cow, you'll never look at a gallon of milk the same way, and the same goes for millions of tasks on the homestead.

Nothing breeds appreciation like knowing the hard work that went into providing our family with something.

I think this also correlates very closely with the homesteading mantra: "Use it up, wear it out, make it do, or do without". When the items that one grows or produces holds such extreme value, they tend to be treated far better and made to last, as well as utilized to their maximum. It's hard to find homesteaders that are wasteful – they appreciate the value of everything (even if it's garden scraps or manure for the compost pile).

HOMESTEADING ADDS A NEW VALUE TO MEAT:

If you've ever grown your own your own meat, you know two things: 1. Meat takes an incredible amount of energy (ie: feedstuff) to raise and 2. Taking the life of the animal you are raising for meat is hard.

Let's start with the first point – the amount of energy it takes to raise meat. Whether this be in the form of grass or grain, the amount it takes to raise the mean is quite astounding. Because of this, we've found that the amount of meat that we eat has been greatly affected. We don't eat it at every meal. We don't even eat it every day. Limited resources of energy in the form of feed means limited amount of meat. Because vegetables and eggs can be grown here with such fewer resources than meat, that's a huge portion of what we eat. They are easier, cheaper, and require less energy to produce. Not something one really has to think about when purchasing meat from the store, but for a homestead, it's a really important equation to consider.

Taking the life of our meat animals also adds a new value to eating this protein. As was the case with our rabbits and our chickens, it was with great sadness and a profound appreciation that we slaughtered and butchered them for our consumption. It's not something to be taken lightly and when we've actually had to do the raising, killing, and processing of the animals ourselves we've found the meat to be far more valuable to us. You can read more about why we morally agree with eating meat HERE.

Homesteading develops a truer sense of gender roles

We hold to a Biblical view and belief of gender roles and life on the homestead has proven those gender roles to be so true and necessary. Stuart is so strong and capable of many of the manual labor tasks that I am physically incapable of. I wish I was buffer – but I ain't. And so it goes. While nursing Owen, catering to nap schedules, preserving food, and preparing meals, I find myself naturally more drawn to work in the home (or that which can be done in the garden or in the coop with the children). While this isn't always the case (as I often lend Stuart a hand with big projects, bucking hay, or building fence) it's given me a new appreciation for my role as a Christian woman and as a wife, helpmeet, and mother.

I see great value in the chores that not only keep this homesteading running but also are of great service to this family

Life on the homestead has caused me to see how these roles became so defined in times past – I picture a woman with a child on each hip, a giant white apron smeared with kitchen projects, and a few chickens following her around the yard. It's a beautiful thing and in no way less meaningful or important. All work on the homestead is extremely valuable and all of it is required to keep it running smoothly. Someone's gotta milk. Someone's gotta cook biscuits for breakfast. And someone's gotta butcher the animals.

HOMESTEADING INCREASES KNOWLEDGE:

Like anything you commit time and energy to, naturally, knowledge is gained on the subject matter. Running a homestead has been no different. We've learned about everything from native grasses, to feed conversions, to heritage breeds, to the patterns and cycles of the honey bee, to milking a dairy cow, to fencing options, to soil assessments, to composting, to pollination, to cheese making, to water and energy usage, to first aid, to gutting a chicken, and everything in between.

One year ago, I had no idea how to do almost all of the homesteading tasks that I am capable of today. And we all remember my first experience hand milking a cow, don't we?

Knowledge is gained from other homesteaders, the internet, a variety of books (such as THIS, THIS, or THIS), and hands on work. It's a steep learning process full of common sense and practical knowledge.

Homesteading breeds dreams:

As of yet, we've never found that nirvana of perfection

with our homestead. We're always looking forward to what we can do better, more efficiently, and with improved results. Once we are successful with one project, it's time to expand the operation and dream bigger!

I love to dream. It's one of my favorite past times. It keeps us working and hopeful for what is to come!

While these great benefits of homesteading may not be true for every homesteader, we've found them to be very true to ours. At the risk of sounding cliche, homesteading has developed our character and grown us into better people of faith. We rely on the Lord for all the happenings every day on the homestead and are so thankful for every day that we get to continue on this journey with our land and our animals.

STEPS TO START A HOMESTEAD

1) Evaluate Your Property

Every property will come with its unique strengths and challenges. When you first set out to start a homestead – what type of property are you working with? Do you already own land, or are you still on the hunt to find a slice of Earth to call your own? Are you currently in your forever home, or do you hope to move again someday soon?

Temporary vs Forever

While you will not want to invest a huge amount of money or energy into a rental or temporary space, don't let it stop you from practicing at least some homesteading activities! For example, when we lived in rental accommodations, we still built a couple of raised garden beds. We also grew food in containers, and started composting. This small introduction enabled us to learn some basics of gardening before buying our first home. Just be sure to check with your landlord before doing anything too permanent.

We know this current property isn't our forever home, but we certainly haven't let that stop us from enjoying it to the fullest while we are here! Before we were able to have an extensive garden, we stocked up on seasonal produce at local farmers markets to practice various food preservation techniques. You can also learn to sew, craft, brew kombucha, or make homemade sourdough – no matter your living situation!

A four part image collage showing what one can do in a rental property with limited space. The images vary from getting the necessary supplies to build raised beds such as wood and soil, filling the raised bed with soil once it is built, planting out the raised beds with various plants of choice, in this case it was tomatoes, squash, peppers,and basil, and finally using containers to grow vegetables. They can easily be moved and don't take up as much space.

Our garden in the last rental house we lived in before buying this home. We snuck in two raised beds where there was space, found random patches of soil to amend and plant strawberries and flowers directly in the ground, and used a few containers too!

Size, Restrictions, & Layout

Now, think about the property size. A modestly-sized property will be more manageable in regards to maintenance, but may also limit the activities you can do on it – such as what types of animals you can raise. Goats, cows, or pigs would not be happy in our 1/5 acre town lot. Nor could we legally keep them! Be sure to familiarize yourself with your town regulations regarding livestock, poultry, bee-keeping, or even things like having a farm stand or collecting rainwater if those are things you're interested in doing.

Now, assuming you do have some property to work with...

it's time to make the most of it! Before diving into any permanent projects, be sure to take time to sit back and observe first. For example, you should evaluate an area's sun exposure and source of shade before installing a veggie garden. Also keep in mind how the sun's path will change with the seasons.

Spend time wandering about in your space. How do you want it to eventually look, feel, and function? While nothing needs to be set in stone now, try to dream up your optimal layout – which should be convenient and functional.

A great example of a thoughtful and purposeful layout is through permaculture design, as shown below. You won't want your farm animals directly next to the house. They may be stinky or noisy! Yet you don't want them so far away that it becomes a trek to go visit and care for them, especially if you live in an area with cold winters. Something you will visit frequently, such as a kitchen herb garden, would be ideal just outside the front or back door. Keep your compost area fairly accessible, but not outside your bedroom or kitchen window. I think you get the idea

In permaculture design, there are zones by use and intensity. Zone 0 = The home and kitchen. Zone 1= Highly accessible kitchen garden, areas frequently visited and maintained. Zone 2= Often visited, a good place for chickens and additional food production. Zone 3 = Fruit trees and larger grazing farm animals. Zone 4 = Increasingly wild food forest and animal forage area. Zone 5 = Wild, unmaintained, and rarely visited.

MAKE A LIST OF PROJECTS & IDEAS

If you're dreaming to start a homestead, two types of thoughts are likely going through your head. 1) You're fantasizing about all of the wonderful, healthy, uber-rewarding things that this new lifestyle will bring you. And it will! I promise. But 2) You are also fretting over all the skills, tools, money, time, or other resources you may not have to make all of those dreams come true right now. Here is the deal: pretty much no one does. Not right at first, and not all at once!

Before you read my example idea list below, please know that it is NOT intended to add to the feeling of overwhelm! Yet for me, it feels good (great, actually!) to get all of the ideas swimming around in my head OUT and down on paper. I find it easier to focus, and then narrow down or prioritize what is next, which is exactly what you'll have to do.

Example Homesteading Projects & Goals

Create a veggie garden space

Plant an herb garden

Plant fruit trees or an orchard

Start a compost area, worm bin, compost tumbler (or all of the above)

Create a pollinator bed, area, or even a meadow full of flowers

Learn how to ferment, can, dehydrate and/or pickle your harvests

Adopt chickens, goats, sheep, rabbits, pigs, cows, or other "farm animals"

Build a barn, stables, or other auxiliary structures

Create a root cellar or large pantry

Learn how to make kombucha, homemade sourdough, apple cider vinegar, homemade seasonings, vegetable (or bone) broth, and other useful staples

Learn how to make natural medicine like Fire Cider and Elderberry Syrup, or personal care products like calendula oil, soap, lotions.

SO many great ideas, right?!

While great to have dreams and goals, let's take a step back first.

A hand is holding a National Wildlife Federation Certified Wildlife Habitat plaque in front of a view of the front yard garden. There isn't a lot of open space with many plants for pollinators, raised beds for vegetables, shrubs, and trees spaced throughout the area.

A wonderful long-term goal is to turn your property into an ecosystem of its own. But there are usually many smaller (manageable) projects and steps along the way to get there!

3) Prioritize

Now take just one or two manageable projects at a time, and forget everything else on the list for a while. It is 100% unrealistic (and 7000% stressful) to try and do everything at once, within a year, or even within a couple of years! That is, unless you are diving in to start a homestead full-time with unlimited resources and help.

Where to begin? Well, your priorities are personal. This journey to start a homestead is all about what you want to do, and when you want to do it. There are no rules!

Will this simply be a hobby homestead, or do you intend to make a living from your land? That will obviously influence how seriously or quickly you approach projects, and which ones to focus on first. For example, do you hope to sell eggs locally? Then building a secure chicken coop and establishing a flock will be at the top of your list.

Certain homestead projects will dictate the order or timeline for others. For instance, you shouldn't set up a beehive until you have a healthy pollinator garden, orchard, or other nectar and pollen-producing plants established first.

Circumstance will also drive your priorities. Like: "Oh crap, the irrigation line broke! I guess it is time to brush up on our plumbing skills..." Or that moment when your kitchen counter is overflowing with homegrown tomatoes, but you've never preserved tomatoes before. Evidently, the time to dive in and learn is now!

DeannaCat is cradling four chicks between two hands and hers torso. Two of the chicks are golden brown in color while the other two are black and white. Chickens can be an important step when deciding to start a homestead.

For me personally, getting baby backyard chickens was a top priority when we first bought this home.

If I had to recommend three homestead projects to focus on first, they would be: create a small vegetable garden, plant trees, and think about irrigation. Edible and/or ornamental trees are a quintessential part of a productive homestead, but they can take a long time to grow! The sooner you get trees planted, the sooner they'll mature to provide food, shade, and privacy. The trees and garden space will both need water, so establishing a functional irrigation plan is also key!

The next step I highly encourage is to start composting, even on a small scale. The goal of starting a homestead is to be self-sufficient and sustainable, and compost pretty much screams both of those things. Close the loop and up-cycle kitchen scraps or garden trimmings into free rich organic fertilizer. Homemade compost (aka "black gold") is invaluable and will significantly boost the fertility of your garden! Soil health is everything. Check out this Compost 101 article to learn about 6 different ways you can compost at home, or learn how to create and maintain simple worm compost bin here.

DeannaCat standing with a potted avocado tree in the Homestead and Chill gardens, about to plant the tree

Two hands are cradling a mound of red wriggler composting worms. There is a plastic bin in the background and a tub full of hydrated coconut coir that will be used to start a worm composting bin.

Say hello to your best homestead friends.

Never Stop Learning

Now that you have your priorities straight, it is time to do a bit of research on the task at hand! Personally, I feel that anything worth doing is worth doing right. I'm not saying to overthink every tiny detail or fret over every little what-if; there is definitely something to be said about enjoying the process of "learning by doing"! Yet it is a great idea to become at least somewhat familiar with the ideas that you'd like to implement before diving in.

Let's also be clear about this: mistakes WILL be made! It is normal and expected. Plus you'll learn and grow from them! On the other hand, if you educate yourself on a skill or task first, you may nip a few mistakes in the bud – and prevent potential wasted time, resources, and heartache.

WHERE TO LEARN HOW TO HOMESTEAD

One of the most common questions I get asked is "where did you learn all this stuff?" The answer is: All over the place! Wherever I can! I'll admit that I gained a slight head start in college by choosing to focus on environmental studies and sustainability, but SO much more of what I've learned about homesteading came after that.

Pick up a few good books on subjects of your interest, such as urban homesteading, gardening, raising chickens, bee keeping, herbal medicine, or compost. Cold winter months are an especially great time to read, soak in new knowledge, and plan.

Even better, get up close and personal! Look into local organizations that may offer tours, workshops, or classes. For instance, our local Farm Supply Company routinely hosts free workshops on various incredibly useful topics. We have attended talks about how to plant and prune fruit trees, the basics of keeping chickens, safely canning food, and more. I know our local Master Gardeners chapter does the same.

Last but not least, I'm here to help the best I can! Here are a handful of our foundation 101 articles that

A Beginner's Guide to Using a Hobby Greenhouse

Aaron is inside the greenhouse while it is still under construction. There are tools laid here and there and there are at least two panels of the roof that still need to be installed. A greenhouse is a great use of space to start many plants by seed.

5) Start Small

As you may likely imagine, maintaining a bustling, productive, full-blown homestead can take up a lot of your time! Truth be told, we don't have much of a social life outside of our home and day jobs these days – but we're perfectly okay with that! It is by choice, and we don't view it as a sacrifice. But you need to ask yourself: How much free time do you have, or are you willing to dedicate to your homestead, garden, or animals?

Time commitment aside, starting small will enable you to enjoy the process and give each project your full attention. Personally, I'd much rather take my time on something and feel like I "nailed it!" than half-ass five things at once. Or even worse, start things and never finish them at all.

For instance, I recommended starting a vegetable garden as an early homesteading priority. However, that doesn't mean I suggest building and installing 15 raised beds all at once! Start a small manageable garden area, especially if gardening is new to you – and leave room to expand later. You'll continue to learn as you go, and also get a better idea of what you can realistically keep up with.

What if there is an issue you didn't anticipate? Such as a problem with the soil you used to fill garden beds, or gophers coming from below and eating your crops? Or, if you change your mind about the style or method of a project? It is SO much easier to make adjustments or even completely re-do a smaller space than if you went overboard in your initial pursuit. See what I mean in the photos below.

The idea of "start small" applies to all types of homesteading activities and projects. Maybe consider planting your first garden with nursery seedlings rather than growing everything from seed, or at least a portion of it. Adopt and learn how to raise a handful of chicks, rather than starting your first flock with Master the art of one food preservation skill before tackling them all.

A three part image collage, the first image shows raised garden beds halfway through construction, there are two similar sized patches of dirt where the grass has been removed as a place for the garden beds. The second image shows the garden beds after four of six months of use and there are weeds growing up and around the garden beds amongst the vegetables, the third image shows Aaron removing the soil from the beds because they are infested with weeds and the space needs to be redone to do it correctly. This was a lesson learned through trial and error.

When we first started the front yard garden, we didn't prepare the space well. We simply removed two garden-bed size sections of our super weedy crabgrass "lawn", put the raised beds down (lining the bottom with chicken wire for gophers but no weed barrier), and then filled them with soil. Within just a few months the new beds were getting totally infested with crabgrass. The damp rich soil inside was like a damn magnet. No amount of mulch would keep it down. Thankfully, we "started small" and only had two beds to move and re-do! Yes, we dug all of the soil back OUT of the beds to fix the issue.

A three part image collage, similar to the three just shown, however, this is showing how we corrected our initial mistake. The first image shows Aaron bending a the waist as the dirt and weeds from the final bed is taken out. In the foreground you can see that construction grade weed block fabric has been laid down and the other bed as been refilled with weed free soil. The second image shows the area halfway redone, The four garden beds are in place and the back half of the area is covered in gravel, the front half is still visible which shows the weed block fabric. The third image shows the area once it is completely finished. Raised beds full of vegetables, the surrounding area is landscaped with gravel and paver lined walkways. You must be prepared to correct a mistake when you decide to start a homestead.

Once we removed the soil, we lifted the beds out of the way, removed all of the grass in one half of the lawn, covered the entire area with a layer of thick painters paper then commercial duty weed blocking landscape fabric, put the beds on top of that (plus two little ones relocated from another area), and about three to four inches of 3/8" green rock gravel around them. Note that this type of extensive ground covering isn't necessary or recommended in all situations. I will be writing an article about "how to kill your lawn and grow food instead" soon, which will dive into that idea deeper.

GET COMFORTABLE IN THE KITCHEN

As your homestead (and plants!) begin to grow, you'll need to know your way around the kitchen. Preparing meals with fresh homegrown food is the bees knees, and one of the key components of homesteading! If you aren't already a "natural" in the kitchen – don't worry! Dig in and have fun. While I totally embrace following recipes at times, don't let them restrict you either.

In addition to playing with all that fresh homegrown food, there are times that homesteading outright demands your time in the kitchen – to preserve the excess bounty! When your garden looks like it is ready to burst at the seams with veggies, you'll want to find ways to preserve it. If I had to estimate, I'd say that we eat 65-70% of our homegrown produce fresh, preserve 25%, and the remaining 5-10% is split between the chickens and compost pile – but nothing goes to waste!

"Putting up" your bounty is an excellent way to reap your rewards into the winter, or enjoy something later when it's no longer in season. Preserving food also enables you to enjoy your homegrown goodies in a different way, such as a seasoning or condiment, which keeps things interesting and palatable!

There are many methods to preserve homegrown food, including: fermentation, dehydration, freezing, canning, vinegar pickling, or even extending shelf life via simple cold storage. We rely on the first three listed the most.

Our Top Homestead Preservation Recipes:

Simple Roasted Tomato Sauce (freeze or can)

The Besto Pesto: Lemon Walnut Parmesan Basil Pesto (freeze)

Allllll the dried seasonings, such as homemade garlic powder, onion powder, chili powder, turmeric powder, and lemon peel powder (dehydrate)

Super Green Sauerkraut (fermented)

Various veggie "pickles" like dilly green beans, radishes, carrots, and beets (fermented)

Apple Cider Vinegar (fermented)

Sweet & Spicy Pepper Sauce (fermented)

A four part image collage, the first image shows seven pint jars of roasted tomato sauce lined up and ready to freeze for preservation. The second image shows a hand holding a half pint mason jar full of freshly made pesto sauce while three full jars sit in the background. The third image shows a glass crock full of apple chunks, water, and sugar which is the start of making your own apple cider vinegar and the fourth image shows five pint jars of different seasonings, they are oregano, onion powder, lemon powder, chili powder, and garlic powder. There are two half gallon mason jars in the background full of dried chilis. Preserving your harvest is a key step to start a homestead.

7) Adding "Farm" Animals to Your Homestead

Not all homesteaders raise animals, but it is more common than not. Ducks, goats, cows, sheep, chickens, rabbits, pigs, quail, llama… the list goes on. Animals can serve many purposes – beyond being raised to eat!

We are vegetarian, so I won't be able to teach you much about raising animals for meat. Our chicken's eggs provide us with a nutritious and organic source of home-raised protein. However, we see our chickens as beloved pets and friends first and foremost. We'd also love to raise goats for milk and cheese one day, but only when we have enough time and space – which definitely isn't now! Other vegetarian homesteaders keep rabbits as companions. Plus, bunny poo is a wonderfully rich but mild natural fertilizer.

A wire basket is full of an assortment of fresh eggs. They range in color from light brown, to blue, to light green, to dark brown.

More than a few things to consider with animals…

If you are interested in adding animals to your new homestead, I beg you to do your research first. Above and beyond any other homestead project, it is your responsibility to thoroughly educate and prepare yourself to care for your animals. Make sure you know what you're getting into, and that you can make the commitments required to provide them a safe and comfortable life. Each type of farm animal has unique needs, but they also each have a lot in common.

Providing secure, clean, and predator-proof housing should be a top priority. This is true no matter if you're living in the country or an urban setting, and particularly important for small and vulnerable animals like chickens. I can't tell you how many people have contacted me completely heartbroken and shocked after a "predator incident" with their chicken flock. The worst part is, 99% of the cases were preventable with better predator-proofing.

Other things to consider are: the animal's dietary needs, daily or weekly care routines, waste management (read: poop), local regulations, and ranging space required. Also, do you have a plan for when you go away on vacation? Is there a local specialty veterinarian to call on when they get sick? Are you comfortable jumping in to help during emergencies?

I don't mean to dissuade you from bringing home some farm animals! Just be prepared, please.

DeannaCat is standing amongst a sea of green with trees and flowering perennial and annual plants surrounding her. She is clutching a wicker basket full of freshly harvested apples. In the foreground, there are three chickens pecking around on the stone lined "pollinator island".

I love these dang birds… but they do cause us some extra work, plus effort and creativity to provide them ample free range space without destroying the gardens!

Get Crafty & Thrifty

The journey to start a homestead may push you out of your

comfort zone in many ways – which is one of the things I love about it most! Don't be afraid to get crafty, creative, and build things you never have before. DIY projects can help you save money, add character to your homestead, and are always an excellent learning experience – frustrations and all!

Trust me, when we first started our homesteading journey, I did not consider either of us handy... at all. Sure, I always liked to sew or do crafts, but actually building things? Nada experience. We even attempted to build our very first raised garden bed using a hammer and nails instead of screws and a drill. It was 1000 times more laborious and far less sturdy than our future garden beds. Lesson learned!

DeannaCat is shown kneeling down taking a measurement of a partially made wooden raised garden bed. Constructing garden beds and structures may be a necessity when on decides to start a homestead.

SAVING MONEY ON HOMESTEAD PROJECTS

The cost of projects is often a big concern for new homesteaders. Thinking outside the box can definitely make things more affordable. Be an opportunist. Seek out used or discounted materials, equipment, or tools online, on Craigslist, Nextdoor, at thrift stores, or local yard sales. Many of our ceramic garden pots, harvest baskets, mason jars, and other kitchen goodies are thrifted.

Another awesome way to save money (and be sustainable!) as you start your homestead is to up-cycle things you already have. Our chicken coop is made of about 70% up-cycled wood that we found in the rafters of our garage when we moved in. It was the first "structure" I ever designed and built!

There is one caveat here. Sometimes it is worth buying the "right" materials for the job rather than sacrificing durability or quality by using something cheap. For instance, it may be really inexpensive to build a raised garden bed with used fence boards or pallets from Craigslist… but how long will it last? Or, is that wood potentially pressure-treated and toxic? Having to replace garden beds in a few years (as opposed to the decade-or-longer lifespan of cedar or heart redwood raised beds) may actually cost you in the long run. Similarly, be smart and recognize when it is worth hiring a professional contractor to help with high-risk jobs.

A three part image collage, the first image shows the chicken coop n mid construction. There is a plywood floor with a plywood side and nest boxes hanging off of one end. There are 2x4's running along each side in different directions for support of the structure. There are 4x4's protruding out of the bottom of the coop which are the legs and feet of the coop. The second image shows DeannaCat on a small step ladder nailing roof shingles to the top of the chicken coop roof. The third image shows the coop and run once fully complete, there is hardware cloth predator proofing lining the run and underneath of the coop.

Our mostly up-cycled scrap wood DIY chicken coop. The windows are made from thrift store picture frames. Isn't she cute? The perfect size for 2 to 6 hens. We have always had 4.

The coop and chicken run are shown once again after a few years of use and a new paint job on the coop. Both structures remain sound in their construction and have kept out all predators to date.

The coop now. I gave her a fresh coat of paint and new cobblestone border a couple years back.

9) Have Fun

Last but not least, my final bit of sage advice to instill in you is this: don't forget to enjoy the process. Isn't the whole idea to start a homestead and leave some of the "real life" stress behind, slow down, and stop to smell the roses?! Remember that Rome wasn't built in a day, and nor will your new homestead be.

When you see the timeline of how we transformed our home into a homestead below, you'll notice that we focused on just a couple projects per year. I personally loved spacing it out. Not only was that the only realistic way for us to approach it, but it kept me excited and busy – for years! Taking your time means you always have something to look forward to and plan. Honestly? It is far less exciting now that all of the big projects are mostly done.

While you're busy planning where the gardens, chickens, bees, and trees will go, don't forget to create space for yourself too! Add places to relax around your homestead, such as outdoor benches, tables, or a fire pit. Create interest and a touch of whimsy with garden art, sculptures, or other things that bring you joy. Make the space inviting after dark with the addition of solar lights. Take time out to pat yourself on the back and admire your hard work.

The backyard patio is shown during dusk. There are two beers on the patio table and the string lights that line the eaves of the house are lit. When one starts a homestead, it is a good idea to take time for yourself and relax on occasion.

We always make sure to relax and reconnect after a long day working in the garden. One of our favorite ways to unwind is to grab the Firefly, put on some music, pop a kombucha, and play a game of cribbage by the fire.

OUR JOURNEY TO START A HOMESTEAD

People are always quite curious about how we turned our very average, fairly barren .19 acre beach town lot into a thriving mini-farm. The answer is: with hard work, patience, and love!

To be honest, I don't think we ever said "let's start a homestead". It simply started with two garden beds and a chicken coop, and naturally continued to grow and evolve from there. We fell in love with the process of planning and working on outdoor projects together, and simply kept going until we ran out of space and projects to do. We've also put almost all of our energy into the outside of our home rather than inside – which definitely needs some major love too!

How we prioritized & budgeted for projects

It became a routine to tackle two "big projects" per year, usually about 6 months apart. That is just what worked well for us! You might not be surprised to hear that my mind never stops going, and neither of us like to sit still much. Our mild climate also allows us to work outside year-round. The bulk of the work was done from 2014 to 2018.

I'm sure you may be wondering about budgeting, so here is the scoop: First of all, we don't spend much money outside the home except for bills and necessities. I am not a big shopper. We don't go out to eat, go to the movies or other spendy activities, and travel very rarely. Additionally, we have done everything DIY – except for replacing the roof. Remember, know when it's best to call in the pros!

Even so, we usually could not afford to save up several thousand dollars at once for a big garden project. But then we found out about the Home Depot consumer credit card and its special promotions. Not to encourage anyone to go into debt! But I want to be honest, and it did help us achieve our goals. When you spend a certain amount on the card at once (usually $500, 1000, 2000, etc) you can qualify for a corresponding interest-free period (either 6, 12, 18, or 24 months, depending on how much was spent). Then we'd pay off that project within the interest-free time frame BEFORE starting the next one. We knew we had the means and diligence to do this.

HOMESTEADING SKILLS TO LEARN FIRST

Gardening

This is the skill you would expect to see on the list, and for good reason. Every bit of food you grow or raise yourself is one less bit you would have bought from the grocery store. I am not against grocery stores! I am for being self sufficient. It is nice to know how to grow food because it tastes great, is as fresh as you can get, and you know exactly what was used to grow it. Since most of us have other jobs in addition to our homesteading efforts, grocery stores are very convenient to have around. And should some type of emergency happen, financially or otherwise, you will know how to grow your own food.

Home grown food can be used to barter, trade or help someone in need. My advice is something I try to follow. Start with a manageable size garden. If you work off the homestead, your garden efforts will be largely concentrated on the weekends. Trying to plant, weed, water, and tend to a large plot of ground every weekend will be exhausting, unless it is your favorite thing to do. Grow a smaller amount at first. In some zones, a fall garden will offer a way to get more produce. Succession planting is another method to increase yield from a smaller garden.

Know your garden zone and purchase plants and seeds that do well in your climate. When you have a plant that is doing well for you and is from heirloom seeds, learn to save seeds from those plants. These seeds from top performing plants can be used the next season in your garden.

HOMESTEADING SKILLS

Cooking

As important as growing food, knowing how to cook healthy food is one of the important homesteading skills. Don't worry if you have been relying on take out food and restaurants for your meals. Cooking is nothing more than following a plan. The internet has many cooking websites that you can access. Purchase one comprehensive cook-book that uses real food ingredients and read through the recipes. Its not as hard as it looks! When you grocery shop, purchase whole ingredients such as meat, cheese, fresh vegetables, whole grain and natural bread products. Better yet, try an easy no – knead bread recipe and bake your own bread

Heating

Learn to chop firewood safely. A chainsaw will make the job easy if you know how to safely operate one. Or learn to use an axe. Either way, if you need an alternate form of heat, wood fire is your answer. It may even become your only source of heat.

Maintain your fireplace or wood burning stove so it operates safely and efficiently. Get your stores of firewood in place during the summer so you have seasoned wood ready when the weather turns cold. Any wood will burn, but wood that has been stacked correctly and seasoned or weathered, is drier and will catch fire quicker. Green wood can be a challenge to many people trying to start a fire for warmth.

Hunting and Foraging

Yes, I realize that these are two entirely different topics but for this purpose my intention is to highlight wild food. Learn what is edible and how to find it, prepare it, and cook it. If hunting isn't for you, there are plenty of wild plants in rural areas that can supplement your food supply. Wild berries picked during the season, can be preserved by canning, freezing or dehydrating. Greens and herbs are often plentiful. Have a reliable field guide that can help you identify plants and berries. My rule of thumb is if I can't clearly identify something, I leave it behind. Some wild foods can make you sick, if consumed.

If you choose to hunt for game animals, learn the proper seasons for each species. Check the laws for your area about licensing requirements. Keep your weapon clean and prepared and store it in a safe manner.

Healing

Using natural plants such as herbs to create health promoting mixtures is a natural step from cooking with whole foods. Herbs are very easy to grow indoors and out. Homegrown herbs can be added to your home cooked meals as seasoning and flavor. Infusing oils from the herbs is an easy step that takes very little time. From the infused oils, beeswax, coconut oil, and olive oil, it is easy to create homemade salves, lotions and soaps. When you use these products you made, you know that they include only fresh ingredients and no harmful chemicals.

Honey is one of the best healing products. Even if you don't have your own bees, you can get raw honey from other farmers, or suppliers. Try using honey in mixtures or straight from the jar. Colds, coughs, skin rashes, burns, and more ailments can be healed with the help of raw honey. It is definitely one of the best things to learn more about and a valuable addition to your homesteading skills.

Sewing

When you know how to sew by hand, you can repair clothing, towels, bedding and more. Instead of buying new, you will be able to repair your favorite barn shirt. Making something useful will become easy for you with just a little practice. Quilting uses sewing skills to take bits of fabric from different sources and combine them into a usable new item. Quilts are also a thing of beauty for your home.

Sewing skills can be used to repair livestock coats, like those used on horses and sheep. Being able to repair costly items can save you considerable money.

Advantages of Homesteading Your Property?

Property Taxes

A homeowner's understanding when it comes to homesteading her property most often has to do with the property-tax exemption. Generally, this advantage of homesteading pertains to shielding a portion of a home's value from property taxes. Often, a typical homesteading advantage is that it'll exempt the first $25,000 to $75,000 of a home's assessed value from all property taxes. With a $50,000 homesteading exemption, you'll only owe property taxes on the home's remaining assessed value.

FORCED SALE IMMUNITY

With a homestead exemption, your home is shielded from a forced sale to satisfy creditors. For example, the lender financing your automobile can't force the sale of your home if you default on your auto loan. Before homestead exemptions, creditors could and often did try to seize a homeowner's property to satisfy all kinds of debts. Homestead exemptions, however, don't normally shield your home from forced sale in mortgage foreclosures or from defaulted property taxes.

Surviving Spouse Advantages

California's own homesteading laws work to protect the homestead interests of surviving spouses by guaranteeing their homesteading rights. State homestead laws vary, but surviving spouses under homestead laws retain the homestead right to their homes for life. For surviving spouses, as long as they use and occupy the homesteaded property, they won't lose homestead rights. Surviving spouses on homesteaded properties, though, must make any mortgage and other payments due in order to retain their homesteading rights.

Homestead Requirements

In order to declare a homestead on your home, it must be your principal residence. In California, homestead exemptions apply only to real property. You won't be able to declare your house boat or motor home a homestead under certain state's homesteading laws. Your homestead exemption and its advantages last until you effectively abandon the homestead, too. Commonly, you abandon an old homestead when you declare another home your new homestead.

Important Things You Should Know Before Starting a Homestead

How Self-Sufficient Do You Want to be?

This is the most important aspect to consider before launching your homestead.

Some people just want to grow their own vegetables with self-sufficient gardening. Others want to raise their own animals. Some take it even further and want to be even more independent and have a complete self-sufficient living lifestyle, by living totally off the grid. It is important to have a goal in mind before getting started so you can create a more accurate plan.

If after you achieve the goals set and decide you want to take it a step further, go for it! However, having that initial goal is so important for motivation in the beginning.

2. Gardening: How do I Make This Plant Grow?

If you are starting a homestead, you need to know how to start something from a seed and make it produce. It is all about how to produce healthy plants that can feed you and/or your family with as little dependence upon the outside world as possible.

You'll need to do lots of research to decide which methods you would like to try.

For instance, you can choose to till your garden or apply the no-till gardening method where you pile your compost and woodchips on top of the soil and let it compost. You can choose to use pesticides or go completely organic.

It is your homestead so you have the freedom to decide what works best for you.

PRESERVING YOUR FOOD

Most people go into the lifestyle of homesteading because they want to know that they can survive regardless of their circumstances. Whether you are concerned about a time that there will be no grocery store available and you should be capable of survival cooking, or tough financial times, being able to grow and then preserve (i.e. can) your own food are some of the most essential parts to homesteading.

It is important to learn how to process your food safely.

You will also need to know what materials you will need in order to preserve your food so that way you can begin stocking up on them.

When canning your food you will need lots of Mason jars. You will also need lids and rings to seal the jars. A pressure canner is an essential part of canning so that way you have the option of pressure canning or water bathing in order to preserve.

Then there is a matter of finding and perfecting the best recipes to save your food in the tastiest way possible.

4. Start Searching for Land

It is important to understand you can homestead on a full fledged farm with acres and acres or something as small as a half-acre or less. You will need to go back to step one and assess how far you want to go to determine how much land you think you will need.

If you want a milk cow obviously you will require more land. If you think you just want a garden and some chickens, you can get away with having less land.

The most important thing to understand when searching for land is that everything must have its place. When looking at land, map it out and see if everything will fit.

You will be surprised at how little land homesteading can actually take. You can also research and find that there are still some areas that give away free land.

When searching for land, it is also a good time to decide what type of home you want to go along with the land. Some people are choosing to build inexpensive tiny houses, others buy old mobile homes or RVs and fix them up, and some choose to place their dream house on their dream land.

The main thing is to map everything out to be sure you can fit all that you want in that space and leave yourself with a little room to grow.

. Learn to Build Anything and Everything

When homesteading, it is important to develop carpentry skills, but you don't have to be an expert. You will soon learn that functional homesteads are not always pretty, and they don't have to be.

However, if you know how to build things you will save yourself a lot of money. You will be able to upcycle many items as well. Carpentry is what will give your homestead character.

6. Research Livestock

A lot of homesteaders choose to raise livestock. This can range from a cow to goats, chickens, ducks, rabbits, pigs, honeybees, and so much more. Research all that homesteaders actually raise. You will be surprised!

Then it is important to learn all about keeping as many animals as you fancy. It is trial and error when keeping animals, but the more knowledge you have beforehand the less painful the learning curve will be. For instance, many people don't know that you can raise chickens and get eggs without a rooster.

This is important to know because if you just want to raise chickens for eggs then you won't have to worry about buying a rooster. However, if you want to raise chickens to hatch then you will need to make the investment and buy a rooster.

7. Upcycling

Homesteading is all about utilizing EVERYTHING! You will be amazed at how much you currently waste once you begin this journey.

Scraps are now compost that can be fed to the animals or used for dirt.

Chicken manure and rabbit droppings are now fertilizer.

Ashes from the fireplace are now thrown out on the garden

to enrich the soil for better growing in the spring.

I can't stress enough the importance of researching through the internet. You will find all kinds of amazing ideas that people have used to upcycle items that are able to meet a legitimate need for little or no cost to them.

8. Equipment…and Pallets

You will need very little equipment to get started homesteading. You will need the basics like hammer and nails. As time goes on you may consider investing in an old tractor, tiller, and other tools that might make your life easier.

However, I don't recommend purchasing a lot before you get started because your plans will change. You will make many mistakes and learn what works.

With that being said, you will find that you will need different things. So make sure you have the basics in order to build with but not much more.

Do start stocking up on pallets.

You can find them for free at many businesses. They are magnificent, cheap items that can be used to build pallet fences, make gates, buildings, walkways, and a lot more. They are usually very sturdy and a great thing to have on hand when you need to build something and don't want to waste money on different materials.

. Money…Don't Sweat It

Homesteading is an investment. However, do not let the financial side of things stress you out.

Many people think that they have to have all of this money upfront in order to go about starting a homestead. That is incorrect so please don't go take out a massive loan to fund your journey. Homesteading is about simplicity so don't complicate it.

Yes, it will take some money to develop your homestead but take it a project at a time.

Homesteading takes time so even if you wanted to fund it all upfront, good luck getting it all done that fast.

Develop a plan (see step 1) and take it one step at a time. This is a lifestyle so it will take patience and ingenuity, but you will be amazed at the homestead you can create for very little money.

FRUITS YOU CAN EASILY GROW ON YOUR HOMESTEAD

Everybody has a different goal when it comes to homesteading. Some people like the idea of being able to grow all their own food simply for the old-fashioned, idyllic nature of it all. Some people are trying to prepare for long-term self-sufficiency or guard against natural disasters or emergencies. Others just want to save a bit of money at the grocery store.Personally, I like growing my own food because it is liberating. I like the idea of producing everything that I eat, and while things like vegetables and chicken eggs are easy to produce, fruits have always been my Achilles heel.

However, there are some fruits that thrive in most climates that can be grown with relatively little skill. Regardless of whether you are a newbie to the world of gardening or you have been doing it for decades, you should consider growing these ten fruits on your homestead this year.

1. Cantaloupes

Nothing quite compares to the crunch of a homegrown cantaloupe. These fruits are easy to grow and easy to preserve – but definitely will be hard to share! They have a short date to maturity, with many producing fruit in as little s sixty-five days. Many homesteaders have success when planting cantaloupes via succession planting, growing multiple crops so that they have a consistent harvest throughout the season.

2. Strawberries

Strawberries are an obvious choice on our list of the easiest fruits to grow. This is because they are incredibly versatile, enjoying success regardless of whether they are grown in hanging baskets, in the ground, or in containers.

They prefer well-drained soil and lots of sun. As your strawberries develop, remove any runners that appear. This will help encourage fresh growth and a greater volume of fruiting. We grow our strawberries in raised beds, which helps to combat weeds and maintain proper soil quality and structure.

3. Blueberries

Blueberries love acidic soil, and produce nutritious berries toward the end of summer. These fruits can be grown directly in the ground or in containers, but we recommend growing them right in the ground as a landscaping feature, as they'll produce gorgeous, scented flowers in the spring.

When you select your blueberry bushes, only choose those that are self-pollinating. Otherwise, you will need more than one plant to produce fruit, which can be cumbersome to deal with.

4. Watermelons

Watermelons are so much fun to grow, particularly for small children who have a tendency to over water plants. You really can't overdo it on water for these moisture-loving melons, and they are both delicious and nutritious.

Easy to grow in any garden, watermelon is hardy in zones 3 to 11. This includes a majority of the United States, and you can modify when and where you plant your watermelon to meet the ideal growing season length and conditions for your watermelons.

Raspberries

The raspberry is a homestead classic, growing well in areas that were once ravaged by fire. These opportunistic fruits grow well in acidic soils, and there are both summer and autumn-fruiting varieties. They prefer good drainage and ample sunshine, but can also thrive in the shade depending on the variety you select.

Grower's tip – after you harvest your raspberries, remove any branches that once produced fruit. The ones that are left will provide you with next year's fruit, and the plant won't have to expend extra energy toward repairing old branches.

6. Apples

While some people claim to have success growing apples in containers, I personally find it easier just to care for apple trees when they are planted directly in the ground. Apples prefer well-drained soils and full-sun, and should be pruned every winter to simulate growth.

Keep in mind that if you already have apple trees on your property, they might not produce the kinds of apples you are used to eating from the grocery store. Wild apples are perfectly safe for consumption, but will have thicker outer skins and a more intense, bitter flavor. They are suitable for baking, but otherwise should just be left to your livestock.

7. Pears

There's nothing quite like a pear to add a savory flavor to your dinners or desserts. There are multiple choices when it comes to growing these beauties, too. You can grow them like bushes from dwarfing root stock, or even grow them against a wall or lattice.

Some varieties of pears are self-pollinating, so you will only need one pear tree to be successful. However, raising more than one is definitely recommended, so that you'll end up with tons of fruit. Peaches taste great when canned in syrup as well as when they are frozen, so there's no reason not to plant tons so that you can have enough to snack on during the winter months, too.

8. Plums

Plum trees are super easy to grow, but are often overlooked by homesteaders. However, if you are considering growing fruit on your small farm, you should definitely consider growing plums. These don't have the need for pollination, as most varieties are self-fertile, and will produce plenty of fruit throughout the middle to end of summer.

As you are growing your plum trees, make sure you keep the fruits at least two inches apart. Thinning the fruit will ensure that your fruits develop appropriately and also that you will have a good crop in the following year, too. Consider planting them against a wall or another structure to grow outward as a fan, and always make sure you plant plums in full sunlight.

9. Figs

Figs are sun-loving trees that provide a taste of the Mediterranean to any dish. They have a sweet, chewy flavor that make them ideally for including in salads or side dishes. They also take great on their own, and can be dehydrated and stored for long-term use.

Figs can be grown in containers to help restrict their roots, and this also allows you to overwinter them. This is particularly important if you live somewhere with harsh winters, where your fig trees might not be able to survive a rugged winter outdoors. You can add supplemental compost to ensure that all of the fig's desired nutrients are being provided.

. Peaches

The first-ever peach trees in the United States came from China and thrive in USDA hardiness zones five through eight. They prefer full sun, and while they may not be suited to colder climates, they are an exceptional choice for a fruit tree if you live in an area with a moderate climate.

If you live in an area that is either too cold or too hot to support growing peaches, you should also know that they can easily be grown in containers

. You may want to select a dwarf fruit tree variety, since they will rapidly outgrow their pots otherwise. They also need to be well-watered and planted in a potting mix that contains vermiculite and peat moss to help conserve moisture.

MOST PROFITABLE ANIMALS FOR SMALL FARMS

1 - CATTLE

With a massive market for beef in the U.S. and Canada, raising cattle is at the top of the list for livestock. Not only do you get a decent payout for each animal you raise, but cattle are remarkably low-maintenance. Even better, if you manage to raise them organically, you'll tap into an even more lucrative market for your beef, milk and cheese.

What You Sell: Beef, milk, butter, cheese

Electric Fencing Options: Use electric poly rope for rotational grazing to cut feed costs. String high tensile fencing to secure the outer fence line boundaries of your pasture.

Cattle are the Best Livestock for Small Farms

Whether you raise egg layers or broilers, chickens are perfect income generators for hobby farms that sell to local markets.

2 - CHICKENS

Even before chicken meat, the real money-maker for chickens is their eggs. That's because eggs are so widely used in meal preparation. The constant production of eggs by hens and their breeding capabilities make chickens a fantastic income generator for a small farmer. Once again, you can boost that profit even more by focusing on the organic egg and meat market. Another helpful sales booster is adding a "locally sourced" label to your eggs and chicken meat.

What You Sell: Eggs, chicken meat

Electric Fencing Options: Install a wire mesh fence with an electrified line at the top and another exterior-facing electrified line. Both will help deter predators.

Goats on Small Farms

Goats offer plenty of income opportunities for a smart hobby farmer. Not only can you sell their meat and milk, but they can also be rented out for weed and foliage control.

3 – GOATS

Believe it or not, the market for goat products are on the upswing. First off, know that 65% of the red meat consumed globally is goat meat. Here in North America, goat meat is still a bit of an oddity, but it's catching on fast and there's a big demand from ethnic markets. Beyond that, goat milk and cheese are considered a healthy alternative to offerings from dairy cattle. Gaining organic certification for your goat products will enhance your sales even more.

A special sub-benefit of goats is that you can even rent

them out to property owners. The goats will clear out heavy patches of vegetation. Yes, they'll pay you to let your goats eat!

What You Sell: Milk, cheese, meat, goat rentals (for foliage control), soap

Electric Fencing Options: Goats are climbers, so you need tall, high tensile fences to keep them contained.

Become a Beekeeper

Honey bees offer hobby farmers a hands-off livestock that mostly takes care of itself. Rent whole hives to other farms to properly pollinate their crops.

4 – BEES

Honey bees are a valuable "livestock" that are relatively easy to develop on practically any farm. You can rent them to other farmers for help in pollination or you can use them to help your own crops. Beyond that, locally sourced honey and beeswax are important products for many consumers, especially for those people who regularly battle pollen allergies.

What You Sell: Hive rentals, honey, bees wax

Electric Fencing Options: It's important to protect hives from wildlife that may exploit the honey or the bees themselves for an easy meal. These animals include bears, skunks, squirrels, raccoons, opossums and rats. A small, multi-line enclosure operated with a battery-powered energizer will keep most of these animals away. Be aware that bears may need a stronger deterrent than an electric fence can provide.

Raising Rabbits for Profit

Rabbits are another growing market in which hobby farmers can invest. Aside from selling them as pets, their meat, manure and pelts are in demand.

5 – RABBITS

Another growing market, rabbits generate a number of sales-friendly products for small farmers. Rabbit meat, for example, is considered quite healthy since it's full of protein while being low in calories. Rabbit pelts can be harvested and sold for use in crafts, coats and hats. For the right household, a fuzzy bunny is a welcome addition to the family – so you can create a small side business selling pet-friendly breeds. Lastly, rabbit manure is considered one of the best fertilizers for organic gardens, so don't let that go to waste.

WAYS TO MAKE MONEY FROM YOUR HOMESTEAD

1. Sell homemade preserves

Homemade jam

Providing for your own food needs is a wonderful thing – yet it takes on a whole new meaning when you begin feeding others with wholesome, homegrown food.

If your cooking skills entice you to spend more time in the kitchen than anywhere else in the house, and you are more than proficient in canning and preserving food, then cooking and selling preserves may just be the spoon to your jam.

Those who don't have time to make homemade preserves for themselves will really appreciate the unique flavors that cannot be bought from the store.

2. Dehydrated goods

If your garden happens to produce a bumper crop of cherry tomatoes and you don't know what to do with them, drying them is the most logical answer.

Sun-dried, oven-dried or in the dehydrator, all work well with time and patience.

You could also sell fruit leather too, provided there are enough children nearby to bring it in demand.

3. Expand your garden

If you have a green thumb, growing and selling additional garden vegetables should come with ease.

Once your garden is established, all you have to do is plant more than you need for personal use and scale up from there. Ideally, plant a bunch of perennial edibles and then once established, they should keep producing year after year with minimal input from you. Here's a great list of perennial veggies, fruits and nuts you can grow at home.

4. Make dried herb and spice mixes

Air drying herbs

In a good year, you can harvest a lot of herbs from your garden. In a great year, there will be so much greenery that you won't know what to do with it all!

You can start by drying your herbs, then packaging them in glass jars. Add a cute label and they are ready for the market:

oregano

basil

rosemary

dill

thyme

mint

Plant extra seeds – sell seedlings

Tomato seedlings

If you have a greenhouse and are able to start planting ahead of season, people are always very grateful for tomato and pepper seedlings that can be planted straight in the ground.

The reason being, it brings their tomato harvest that much closer, without all the fuss of waiting for slow-to-germinate seeds.

Herb seedlings are often a best sell at farmers markets, as they can be taken care of indoors, and never

6. Sell broilers or chicken eggs

Raising a flock of chickens is a joyful experience, but it does come with ups and downs. A bunch of chickens can leave you with almost no eggs at all, to way more than you can eat, with plenty to give away.

Eggs are nutritious and delicious, just as the eggshells are too. Keep enough for yourself and sell the rest for a profit.

7. Raise and sell heritage poultry

Guinea fowl

Turkeys, ducks and geese are not as common to raise as chickens, but there is much to be said for their meat – and eggs!

Of course, it all depends on what kind of bird lover you are, and how much land you have, including access to water – if ducks or geese are to thrive.

Not to forget mentioning the most spectacular guinea fowl, fiercely territorial birds that can be loud on occasion, but with eggs ever so tasty and wild.

8. Start a cow – or goat – share

If you are tired of buying your milk in a plastic bottle from the grocery store, think that perhaps others are also bored with the same routine.

Go out on a limb and offer milk in glass bottles, like it used to be. People will love it when the milk is creamy and delicious!

Most people don't have the land, or the time, it takes to raise a cow – or a goat. Start a cow share, and in exchange for raising an animal, you can profit from the extra milk, raw or pasteurized.

9. Sell handmade cheese, butter and other dairy products

Handmade cheese

Once your cow(s) and/or goat(s) begin producing milk, you'll have to grab some new homestead skills and start making aged cheeses, yogurt, kefir, cottage cheese, butter, sour cream and ice cream.

Become an artisan cheesemaker and soon you can start charging even more for specialty cheeses.

People will buy butter for baking and cheese for everyday meals, though you could also bake with your

Make sausage and jerky

Beyond eggs and milk, meat is the next homestead product that fluctuates in abundance. You won't be slaughtering everyday, but when you do, the excess is evident!

Bacon is one item that can easily be smoked and hung. Sausage making comes in next in terms of ease and market-ability.

11. Raise grass-fed animals

If your homestead has the amount of land that it takes to raise cattle and you are ready to get your hands dirty – go for it!

It will, of course, take some knowledge about rotational grazing, choosing the best livestock for your land and handling such large creatures. Again, if you are passionate about it, then it is a great fit.

12. Plant an orchard or berry farm

Apple orchard

Orchards take patience and careful planning if you wish to succeed – and you do.

If you are starting from scratch, make sure to choose the best varieties that work well locally. Bonus points for your trees and bushes being drought tolerant.

For example, when your apple trees start producing, you could sell the fruit directly, invest in a cider press and make juice, make apple cider vinegar, dehydrate apple slices, or even make apple wine!

U-pick farms are family fun too: peach, blueberry, cherry,

you name it.

This isn't an option for the faint of heart, as it takes a considerable investment to get started, but it will provide you with income for decades to come.

13. Sell homemade baked goods

If you are fortunate enough to have a farmers market nearby and you can commit to being there regularly, then you may have a fairly steady source of income at hand.

All you have to do is come up with a product that sells.

Cookies, muffins, biscuits, salty crackers made with home rendered lard or butter. Add in some garden spices or fresh flowers and make it unique.

14. Beekeeping

A homestead beekeeper

If you have bees, chances are great that you'll have much more honey than you can consume in a year, perhaps with plenty of leftover beeswax too.

Selling honey and homemade beeswax candles are two obvious ways to profit from the bees' hard work, bu don't forget about bee pollen and propolis either.

Grow mushrooms

Growing Shiitake mushrooms the traditional way

Even if you have little space to offer to a money-making enterprise, mushrooms may work for you.

Sell them fresh, or dehydrate them. Most of all, grow them because they are so darn good for you!

Oyster mushrooms are wonderful to work with for beginners, move onto shiitake mushrooms from there.

SELLING HOMESTEAD FOOD PRODUCTS

At some point in your homestead business endeavors, you will have to comply with local food safety laws. These will vary from state to state, country to country. Once you know what you would like to sell, investigate what regulations may be standing in your way.

With regards to meat and milk, look into local regulations before committing to any sale. It may be far easier to sell the live animal, than to sell cut and wrapped chicken breasts, for instance.

Raw milk is another debate, many homesteaders will keep a goat or cow for this very reason alone.

Making money on your homestead with creative endeavors

There is much more to keeping money in flow than selling food and perishables. How about selling art, paintings or jewelry? Things that are not only beautiful and artistic, but practical too.

16. Raise animals for fiber

Understandably, your first thought goes to sheep wool, but there is so much more to animal fiber than that.

Imagine rabbits, alpaca, llama, Pygora and Cashmere goats prancing around your farm. They are all so beautiful and useful in terms of clothing ourselves in a natural way.

Even if you do not become interested in processing the fibers into yarn or felt, someone else will – and they can be found online. That being said, outside of local farmers markets, selling raw fleece and handspun yarns is a very decent way to make a living, so long as you are the crafty type.

17. Sell handmade finished items

If you produce fiber and know how to process it: spinning, knitting, crocheting, etc., then you can earn even more for your craftiness.

Knit hats and scarves. Learn to weave and invest in a loom to make larger pieces of fabric for towels, tablecloths and place mats.

18. Handcrafted soaps, lotions and cosmetics

If you are looking to go into a steady business, make something that people use on a daily basis. Soap is something that we use everyday, and we can be quite picky about our favorite ingredients and scents.

19. Mend, sew and make clothing

You don't need to get muddy to turn a profit on a homestead, you can make a little extra cash simply by repairing work clothes that are worked to pieces.

Tan and sell hides

With sheep, goats or rabbits on the homestead, you will have an influx of hides to tan that would otherwise be thrown away.

They can be used to cover benches, or to keep you warm in the winter months. Our ancestors did it, so can we. If this interests you, look into it further and see how you can get started:

21. Carpentry and blacksmithing

In the past, woodworking and blacksmithing were more of a man's trade. Nowadays, more and more women are empowered to take up the hammer and craft beautiful objects out of metal.

If you can take the heat of a hot wood-fired kitchen, working next to a forge will be a piece of cake.

Carpentry extends far beyond home building, it can even include furniture and toy making! If you can believe in the products you create, others will discover value in them too.

While this way of making money is not something you can readily step into (unless you own the essential tools), it can definitely become a lucrative way to create a sufficient stream of money coming into your life.

22. Teach workshops and classes

Have you discovered your passion yet? Or is there something that you are insanely good at? Let people know and gauge whether there is any interest among locals.

Spinning workshops come instantly to mind, learning to bake bread, making ferments and cooking lessons follow closely behind. Perhaps you are a master gardener and have words of green wisdom – and the garden to prove it!

If you have homesteading skills to share, make sure to charge for them, never give everything away for free!

23. Start a blog

To be honest, having the courage to start a blog is one of the best ways to put knowledge of your homestead out there. But truth be told, most blogs fail to make any amount of significant money. This happens for several reasons that we won't go into here.

However, if you think you have the right formula of charisma, energy, creative design and blog tactics, why not give it a try?

Blogging about life on a homestead can be a wonderful way to boost your income outside of the rat-race!

24. Write a book

If you are a writer, know that people are always in search of new and engaging content. Setting the internet aside for a moment, books still hold a special place in every reader's life. They are tangible – you can flip through the pages, books can be taken on hikes out in nature and they are free from a battery life.

Just as you may have homesteading skills to teach, you

may also have plenty of life experiences to share in the form of writing, whether it be fiction, non-fiction, cookbooks, stories for children or even poetry. Books are excellent ways to share knowledge and pass it down from generation to generation.

25. Become a freelance writer

Do you come in from your bountiful garden, grateful to be out of the hot sun with inspiration dripping off your face?

No matter whether you are an introvert, or extrovert, words are just one of the ways we can express ourselves. Some people are better at speaking, others more clever with meaningful strings of words that roll beautifully off their fingertips.

If you like to write, becoming a freelance writer (in any niche!) can be one of the most enticing ways to make a living. Take the first steps by creating a simple website, or blog, then fill it with relevant content.

26. Freelance photography

With a camera in hand, snapping quality pictures around your homestead can be a relatively easy way to make money.

Setting up a shop and selling prints online is one way to create an income flow, another is to sell stock images. Think chickens, garden produce, cute animals, even a pile of compost. Somewhere, "somewhen", people will need a stunning image of a haystack or a steaming pile of manure…

Raise worms

Worm farming

If you have a market for your worms, than yes, you have the base for a successful business. And once you adopt an entrepreneur spirit, anything is possible.

People will buy them for fishing purposes, for vermicomposting, reptile owners, and of course gardeners who are not only interested in the worms themselves, but also in the worm castings.

28. Incubate eggs

If you are in love with tending to chickens, one good way to share your poultry passion with others is to sell day-old chicks.

29. Create and sell compost

If you have the land, you have the power! And you have all the space to create as much compost as physically possible. Not all gardeners are in the lucky situation to have a rotting heap of veggies in their backyard.

30. Cut and sell firewood

Chopping firewood with an axe

When you live on a homestead, keeping a stack of properly seasoned firewood is a priceless skill to learn for life.

Absorb the knowledge for yourself, because when it comes to buying and selling firewood, another person's "seasoning" may mean something different to yours.

If you have excess trees to cut down, more than what you could possibly burn on your own – sell it green (for less money) or season it well and sell it for more!

31. Sell straw or hay

People need hay and straw for their farm animals (feed and bedding quality), just as they need it for their no-dig gardens.

If you have extra bales, chances are that someone will be in need.

Go old-school and put up signs to sell locally, list them in a dedicated Facebook group, let your homesteading friends know – get the word out that you have excess of anything and people will often lend a helping hand, or dollars for what they need.

32. Rent out your land

Say you've got the land, but no animals (or not enough of them) to put on it. Start renting out grazing pastures for neighbors, or allow for a dedicated space of growing crops. It is a akin to sharing your land, only for money.

33. Offer your homestead for events

If you are lucky enough to have mature trees on your property and a picturesque landscape, then take advantage of it!

Offer your land/garden for photo shoots relating to weddings, anniversaries, birthdays. Just be sure to have clear expectations from both parties and create a contract for covering one-off or recurring events.

34. Start a CSA

If you find that gardening and growing food is indeed

your passion and one of the reasons for jumping out of bed every day, then starting a CSA (Community Supported Agriculture scheme) may come very naturally to you.

If you are up to the challenge and enjoy creating a deeper sense of community, success is yours for the asking. Before getting started, make sure you are in it for the long-term and not just for profits.

35. Offer your expertise/tools to other homesteaders

If you have a tractor and implements, consider being a tractor-driver for hire in the nearby area, and help others get the crops in the ground, as well as helping out at harvest time.

CONCLUSION

On one level, the costs of the events at Homestead are easy to quantify.According to historian Les Standiford, the strike cost Carnegie Steel approximately $300,000, or roughly 10 percent of its net profits in 1892. The AAISW estimated that the lockout and strike cost Homestead's workers more than four times that amount in wages, and Pennsylvania's taxpayers spent half a million dollars restoring control of the works to the company and protecting the scab workers.1 On another level, however, these numbers represent only the tip of the iceberg. One reason for the astronomical increases in the company's profits was the decline in wages that was now possible. By removing the right to collectively bargain and destroying the union, the company had effectively destroyed the workers' leverage when it came to protesting wage reductions; Homestead's skilled workers' wages dropped by more than 50 percent as a result. Profits, which jumped 1,000 percent between 1893 and 1899, far outstripped wages in general, the total cost of which increased by less than 50 percent. Charles Schwab, who had succeeded John Potter as Homestead's superintendent, relentlessly cut costs by extracting as much labor as possible from his workers and by replacing men with machines wherever possible.